Bad Boys of the Reef

By Brian Ardel

blue ocean press
florida - tokyo

Copyright© 2018 Brian Ardel

All rights reserved.

This publication may not be reproduced, stored in a retrieval system, or transmitted in any form or by any means, electronic, mechanical, photocopying, recording, or otherwise, without prior written permission of the publisher, except by a reviewer who may quote brief passages in a review to be printed in a periodical.

Published by: blue ocean press, an imprint of Aoishima Research Institute

U.S. (Main) Office

P.O. Box 510818

Punta Gorda, Florida 33951

807-36 Lions Plaza Ebisu

3-25-3 Higashi, Shibuya-ku, Tokyo, Japan 150

Email: contact@blueoceanpublications.com

URL: http://www.blueoceanpublications.com

ISBN: 978-4-902837-42-1 (Hardcover)

ISBN: 978-4-902837-41-4 (Softcover)

A whale family swam my way,

The baby asked if he could play.

Mom said "Yes, but you must teach him Keith.

Protect him while he's on our reef."

The baby whale said "Swim with me.

There are so may sights to see.

Don't be afraid of snapping teeth.

I'll protect you from the Bad Boys of the Reef."

A hungry shark looked me up and down.

Keith said, "Get lost you little clown."

A barracuda came around the bend.

Keith said "Stay away from my new best friend."

An octopus ran when he saw the whale.

Keith laughed and flicked his giant tail.

A dwarf blenny looked really mean,

Even though he was smaller than a bean.

A moray eel snapped then roared.
Keith smiled and looked a little bored.

A jellyfish said, "I'll sting you today."

Keith used his tail to steer us away.

The lionfish had a poison spine.

Keith said, "Stay away, you'll be just fine.

The sea urchin wanted to poke me bad.

Keith led me away, I was quite glad.

Keith said, "The puffer seems a tasty treat,

But he is poison. Do not eat!

The whale shark's the biggest fish on the reef.

But he is friendly. He has no teeth.

The scorpionfish is hard to see,
But he has spines that are deadly.
I bet you didn't see that fish.
Please stay safe, that's my only wish!

A shipwreck looks like a fun place to play,

But it is dangerous. Stay away!

A grouper screamed, "your Dad's looking for you".

Find him fast or you are through.

I couldn't find the boat at all.

The fog rolled in, and I was way too small.

Four dolphins led Dad's boat to me.

Keith said, "Time for you to get out of the sea!

Come back here tomorrow it's my wish.

Then I will teach you to spell with fish!"

www.ingramcontent.com/pod-product-compliance
Lightning Source LLC
Chambersburg PA
CBHW041405010526
44107CB00015B/1078